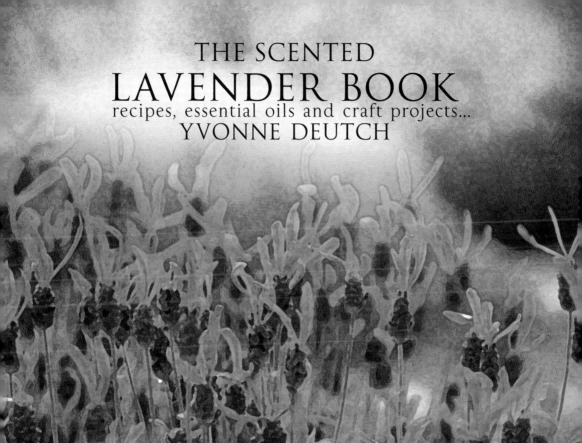

THE SCENTED
LAVENDER BOOK
recipes, essential oils and craft projects...
YVONNE DEUTCH

Picture Acknowledgments:

The publishers would like to thank the following for supplying photographs and illustrations for this book:

The Garden Picture Library: 4, 5, 6, 19, 24, 25, 35, 37, 38, 41, 44, 58, 59, 59-64 (background) • Illustrated London News: 10 (cameo) • Mary Evans Picture Library: 10, 11 • Norfolk Lavender: 14, 15, 16, 18, 21, 22, 48 • Glen Saville: 42 • Deborah Ward courtesy of Virginia McNaughton: title page, 2-18 (background), 19-26 (background), 23, 27-34 (background), 35-46 (background), 40, 46, 47-58 (background), 64

We would also like to express our gratitude to the following Internet contributors:

http://members.aol.com/SonoranNat/fieldguide: 36 • www.artgally.com: 50 • www.artiledesigns.com: 3, 9, 30, 31, 52, 53, 55, 56, 57 • www.aurora-naturalcare.com: 7 • www.countryscentiments.com: 28 • www.fragrant.demon.co.uk: 32, 45, 60, 61, 63 • www.GardenofSoap.com: 49 • www.hydrogarden.com: 8 • www.reneesgarden.com: 2–64 inclusive (corner motif) • www.rowhillgrange.com: 47 • www.sunsetlodge.co.za: 27 • www.wildviolets.com: 50

The author and publishers have made every reasonable effort to contact all copyright holders. Any errors that may have occurred are inadvertent and will be corrected in any subsequent editions if notification is sent to the publishers.

First published in Great Britain in 2002 by Michael O'Mara Books Limited

9 Lion Yard, Tremadoc Road, London SW4 7NQ

A CIP catalogue record for this book is available from the British Library

ISBN 1-85479-869-3

1 3 5 7 9 10 8 6 4 2

Design www.glensaville.com

Printed and bound in Singapore by Tien Wah Press

CONTENTS

The Story of Lavender

K nown and loved for its wonderfully soothing, healing properties, lavender has been a valuable aromatic plant for thousands of years. Its original home is in the mountainous regions of Southern France, and other countries bordering the western half of the Mediterranean. The deliciously scented

shrub was one of the plants recorded in 60 AD by the Greek physician Pedanius Dioscorides. He travelled in the Roman army as a surgeon, and collected information about plant remedies used at that time in his ground-breaking work *De Materia Medica*. This listed the medicinal properties of about 600 plants, and had a profound influence on Western medicine. In 512 AD, a special edition of *De Materia Medica* was prepared for Juliana Arnicia, the daughter of the Roman Emperor Flavius Avicius Olybrius – this contained over 400 colour illustrations, and is the first surviving illustrated herbal.

Lavender was probably known and used even earlier by the ancient Greeks and Egyptians, but it was the Romans who employed it most lavishly, and they were responsible for its spread and cultivation throughout Europe. They held the plant in the highest regard: it was dedicated to Hecate, the Latin name for the Greek goddess of the underworld, and was specially designated to prepare women for childbirth. In this context, the most powerful properties of lavender came into play – its effectiveness in combating infection and encouraging relaxation and, as a magical 'extra', its potent ability to avert the evil eye at this crucial time of vulnerability.

On the march

As their vast empire expanded, the Romans took seeds and cuttings of plants that they considered essential to their health and comfort wherever they settled. In the case of lavender, they used it extensively, both as a highly effective antiseptic, and to scent their baths (lavender derives its name from the Latin word *lavare*, meaning 'to wash').

The Romans were probably familiar with several lavender species, including *Lavandula stoechas*. This pretty little plant has narrow leaves and tiny, dark violet flowers, terminating in a tuft of brightly coloured leaflets. It is a native of the Hyères region of Southern France, which the Romans called the 'Stoechades'. When they conquered Britain in the first century AD, and during subsequent waves of invasion, they seem to have brought different varieties of lavender with them, probably to widen the chances of success in cultivation. Some proved easier to grow than others in the new soil and climate, but *Lavandula stoechas* was one form that survived, and its flowers were used medicinally in England right through to the eighteenth century. This and other species introduced by the Romans such as *Lavandula officinalis* (also known as *Lavandula angustifolia*) and *Lavandula spica* – literally and metaphorically 'took root'.

Going native

Through the centuries following the Roman invasions, lavender became quietly assimilated into local plant lore and usage. During the Middle Ages, it was commonly used as a strewing herb for the floors of churches and houses – to scent the air and mask unsavoury smells, and to repel fleas, insects and lice. It was also burned on bonfires on All Hallow's Eve (31 October) to deflect the malevolent spirits that were believed to be roaming free on that night.

Along with other aromatic plants, lavender was used in a desperate bid to ward off the plagues that swept throughout Western Europe from the fourteenth century onwards. People heard that the glove makers of Grasse in Southern France, who used lavender oil to scent their gloves, were unusually free of the disease. This persuaded thousands to try using lavender against the pestilence, even though the grim truth was that no medical treatment, herbal or otherwise, was able to alter its fatal course.

The great age of herbals

It was the development of the printing press in the fifteenth century that introduced herbal medicine to the wider public. Texts such as Dioscorides' *De Materia Medica*, collated fifteen centuries earlier, were printed for the first time, and this inspired the revival of research and writing on the subject throughout Europe. The sixteenth century, however, was the great age of herbals, which shed fascinating light on how plants were then being catalogued, cultivated and used.

In England, the horticulturalist John Gerard published his treatise *Gerard's Herbal* in 1597. He grew over 1,000 species of plants in his garden – and one of these was lavender. In addition to its traditional virtues as an antiseptic and pest repellent, by Gerard's time it seems also to have gained a reputation for treating various kinds of nervous conditions. 'It profiteth them much,' says Gerard, 'that have the palsy if they be washed with the distilled water from the Lavender flowers, or are anointed with the oil made from the flowers and olive oil in such manner as oil of roses is used.'

Later, in his famous herbal published in 1649, Nicholas Culpeper said that: 'a decoction made with the flowers of Lavender, Horehound, Fennel and Asparagus root, and a little Cinnamon, is very profitably used to help the falling-sickness (epilepsy) and the giddiness or turning of the brain.' He was very aware of the potency of lavender oil, and advised that 'The chymical oil drawn from Lavender, usually called Oil of Spike, is of so fierce and piercing a quality, that it is cautiously to be used, some few drops being sufficient to be given with other things, either for inward or outward griefs.'

Hot lavender

Lavender was certainly known to Shakespeare:

Here's flowers for you;
Hot lavender, mints,
savory, marjoram;
The marigold, that goes
to bed wi' the sun,
And with him rises weeping.'
The Winter's Tale

Shakespeare's reference to lavender being 'hot' was connected with its use in treating colds and fevers. In his herbal *Theatrum Botanicum* (1629), John Parkinson catalogued over 3,000 plant species. With regard to lavender, he said: 'This is usually put among other hot herbs, either into bathes, ointment or other things that are used for cold causes.' He also said that lavender 'is almost wholly spent with us, for to perfume linnen, apparell, gloves and leather and the dryed flowers to comfort and dry up the moisture of a cold braine.' And he commented that lavender is of 'especiall good use for all griefes and paines of the head and brain'.

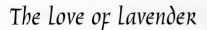

The love of lavender

Lavender was a particular favourite of Queen Elizabeth I. Her palace gardeners were required to have lavender flowers available at all times in order to make Conserve of Lavender (a mixture of lavender flowers and sugar), and sweet lavender tisane, a drink made with lavender flowers, hot water and honey. She also required her ladies-in-waiting to sew sachets of

dried lavender into the hems of their dresses, so that its fresh, piercing fragrance would waft into the air as they walked about the royal court.

The affection that lavender inspired is reflected in *Lavender's Blue* – a traditional English song dating from the late 1600s:

Lavender's blue, dilly dilly,
lavender's green,
When I am king, dilly, dilly,
you shall be queen.

And, of course, the streets of London echoed to yet another musical invocation – the cries of the lavender sellers as they sang out their wares –

'Who'll buy my sweet lavender?'

11

The American colonists

Lavender was one of the plants that the Pilgrim Fathers took with them to America on their historic voyage in the seventeenth century. Its medicinal qualities were widely exploited by the colonists, who used it as a remedy for headaches, convulsions, fainting, colic, laryngitis, and to ease toothache. They also added it to soap to treat skin parasites. And, of course, it was also a favourite herb for strewing about on floors, to repel bugs and other insect pests, and to scent the air.

The apothecary's art

One consequence of the great voyages of discovery and colonization was that travellers and explorers brought back medicinal plants from all corners of the globe. In general, it was the affluent city dwellers who were able to purchase the astonishing range of new products created by specialist apothecaries. Poorer rural people still tended to rely on their home-grown herbs, and would have used simple infusions of lavender for medicinal purposes. Meanwhile, urban shoppers would have been encouraged to buy a concoction known as Compound Tincture of Lavender, sold under the name of Lavender Drops. This was first introduced in 1730, and was sold over the counter as a treatment for faintness.

The preparation later became known as 'palsy drops' and 'red hartshorn'. Its formula appeared in the *London Pharmacopoeia* at the end of the seventeenth century, and was somewhat complicated. It contained nearly thirty ingredients, and was prepared by 'distilling the fresh flowers of lavender, sage, rosemary, betony, cowslips, and lily of the valley in French brandy; in the distillate such spices as cinnamon, nutmeg, mace, cardamoms were digested for twenty-four hours, and then musk, ambergris, saffron, red roses and red sanders-wood were tied in a bag and suspended in the spirit to perfume and colour it.' This concoction was said to be useful 'against the Falling-sickness, and all cold Distempers of the Head, Womb, Stomach and Nerves; against the Apoplexy, Palsy, Convulsions, Megrim, Vertigo, Loss of Memory, Dimness of Sight, Melancholy, Swooning Fits and Barrenness in Women.' A veritable cure-all, in fact.

The modern revival

Preparations such as Lavender Drops later evolved into much more sophisticated modern scientific medicines. Meanwhile, the herbalist's art never completely vanished, though its influence was significantly diminished, and the pathways of botany and medicine had sharply diverged. The botanical books ignored the medicinal properties of plants, while the medical books contained no plant lore. But the cataclysm of the First World War brought a significant change in this process. Trench warfare

resulted in dreadful injuries, and conventional medical supplies frequently ran out. Doctors treating badly wounded soldiers then resorted to using traditional herbal antiseptics, such as lavender, and so saved many lives. This renewed popular interest in herbal remedies was one of the reasons why the eminent English herbalist Mrs M. Grieve compiled her famous work *A Modern Herbal* in 1931. Mrs Grieve grew medicinal herbs in her Buckinghamshire garden. During the war years, when there was a shortage of these plants because they could no longer be imported from abroad, she trained pupils in the work of drying and preparing herbs for the chemists' market. In so doing, she helped to revive the herb industry in England. Her editor, Hilda Leyel, had founded the Society of Herbalists in 1926 at Culpeper House.

Lavender, of course, was one of these plants, and, as Mrs Grieve commented with evident pride and satisfaction, it grew to a rare peak of perfection in English soil. By the time she had completed her herbal, Mitcham in Surrey had already ceased to be the centre of the English lavender-growing industry. The major plantations were in Hitchin in Hertfordshire, Long Melford in Suffolk, Market Deeping in Lincolnshire and in Kent, near Canterbury. As a producer herself, she was keenly aware of the value of the market:

The British Tourist Authority magazine of July 1958, featuring Norfolk Lavender

'The fragrant oil to which the odour of lavender flowers is due is a valuable article of commerce, much used in perfumery, and to a lesser extent in medicine. The fine aromatic smell is found in all parts of the shrub, but the essential oil is only produced from the flowers and flower-stalks. Besides being grown for the production of this oil, lavender is widely sold in the fresh state as 'bunched lavender,' and as 'dried lavender,' the flowers are used powdered, for sachet making and also for pot-pourri, etc., so that the plant is a considerable source of profit.'

In comparing the value of English as opposed to French lavender, she said 'English Lavender is much more aromatic and has a far greater delicacy of odour than the French, and the oil fetches ten times the price.' The English lavender industry continued to prosper, despite being attacked by a fungal disease which caused crops to fail in several areas.

From traditional to modern

One of the most famous English growers, Norfolk Lavender, founded by Linn Chilvers in 1932, has rapidly developed into an internationally known business. Mr Chilvers' father started a nursery garden and florist's business on the north Norfolk coast in 1874.

He supplied plants to Queen Alexandra (wife of King Edward VII) for the Sandringham gardens, and was a Royal Warrant holder. Father and son both had a particular interest in lavender, and grew several varieties. After his father's death, Linn Chilvers started growing lavender on an ambitious scale, so that more and more acres of gently sloping coastal fields became covered with mauve and blue rows of fragrant bushes, shimmering in a misty haze under the clear Norfolk skies.

Norfolk lavender has consistently produced oil of excellent quality and yield and is distilled to ensure maximum purity and quality. The lavender fields have also been kept free of harmful pesticides, so they abound in wildlife. Partridges nest among the bushes, and in summer, the rows of purple and blue flowers are alive with butterflies and bees.

The same applies to the lavender-growing districts of France; visitors find the lavender fields covering the mountain slopes and fields of Provence bewitching. Here, for many years, lavender was gathered from the hillsides by the shepherds and locals who sold it to the perfumiers of Grasse. In the 1950s, however, demand for lavender oil increased and it started to be grown on a commercial scale.

In recent years, to meet an apparently insatiable demand, lavender is grown is such faraway places as China, Tasmania and the USA. Nowadays the modern grower can choose from literally hundreds of varieties that have been developed by plant breeders, each with its own distinct colour, size, shape and fragrance. Ultimately, of course, these all link back to their wild Mediterranean ancestors.

The Scented
Lavender Patch

In her book *Good Country Days*, the post–war country writer Ruth How recorded a luminous episode in her mother's garden; in this fleeting moment, her family's historic link with lavender is brought vividly alive through her mother's memories:

Now in mother's garden we grow lavender again, and the day has come when it seems suddenly to have burst into full bloom, the long hedge a misty, blue-grey cloud of sweetness, deepening into purple shadows.

Lavender tends to evoke strong affections in people. That is not at all surprising, as it can transform a garden into a tranquil, healing place. Simply walking past a row of lavender bushes on a summer evening and quietly inhaling the air will give you a deep sense of calm and inner peace. You don't have to own a large garden to enjoy this simple pleasure; a few pots of lavender grown on a window ledge, or in window boxes or patio containers will bring the same satisfaction.

Growing lavender

Modern gardeners find it very gratifying to discover that lavender is so easy to cultivate. Indeed, its versatility is astounding – this tough, perennial shrub can flourish in the scorching heat of the stony slopes of Provence and, at the other extreme, on the remote Alpine slopes of Norway. However, if you want to provide your lavender plants with the best growing conditions, you should choose a sunny open spot, make sure that the soil is light and well drained, and that it has some sand and lime content. These conditions give lavender the greatest chance to thrive. Once established, it will bloom faithfully year after year.

Give it a good pruning in spring or autumn to prevent straggly growth and bare stems; and check to see if it needs thinning out. Lavender bushes should never be too crowded together. The buds grow on the new growth and will flower from the end of July through to August. You can take stem cuttings in autumn or spring to propagate new plants.

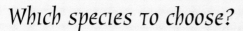

Which species to choose?

The species of lavender that is best to cultivate for home medicinal or culinary use is the classic *Lavandula angustifolia* (also known as *Lavandula officinalis*). The plant has lovely, highly scented, purple flowers, and will grace any setting, from pots to garden borders. This is the one to choose if you need the flowers to make infusions and tisanes.

It's best to use a dwarf variety of *Lavandula angustifolia* to grow in smaller pots: 'Hidcote' or 'Munstead' are good examples. Planting up the fragrant spikes of lavender in pots, window boxes and patio tubs is very easy, and the results can be spectacular.

Shades of lavender

On the other hand, if you can grow lavender on a relatively generous scale, you'll be delighted to discover the astonishing range of colour, shape and size that is available to the modern gardener. Visit a good plant nursery and browse through plant catalogues to see what is on offer.

Depending on the variety, the flowers come in all shades of purple – *Lavandula angustifolia* 'Hidcote', 'Vera', 'Folgate', 'Twickle Purple' and 'Munstead' are just a few examples. They can be a delicate pale pink, as in *Lavandula angustifolia* 'Loddon Pink', or even white (*Lavandula angustifolia* 'Nana Alba').

White lavender used to be a rarity, and is said to have grown in the garden of Queen Henrietta Maria. The seventeenth-century author John Parkinson mentioned white lavender in his writings: 'There is a kinde hereof that beareth white flowers and somewhat broader leaves, but it is very rare and seene but in few places with us, because it is more tender and will not so well endure our cold Winters.'

The leaves of different lavender species provide lots of visual choice, too – they are generally a lovely silver-grey, but vary in how narrow, large and plentiful they are. As for the height of the plant, this can range from 45 cm to 1 metre. You can grow lavender in all sorts of situations – in colourful herbaceous borders, in informal cottage garden plantings, in formal, dense, bushy clumps, as fragrant path edgings, and as a neat little hedge to separate different plots. *Lavandula angustifolia* 'Hidcote' and 'Munstead' are excellent compact, dwarf plants to use for this purpose.

The intense colour and perfume of lavender casts a potent spell over the garden, especially as the flowers reach their peak in late July and early August. They are magnets for honey bees and butterflies, especially tortoiseshells.

Harvesting the crop

Experienced lavender-growers have always been very careful to harvest the plants at the point when they contain their richest yield of essential oil. Mrs Grieve describes the importance of all this in her *Modern Herbal*:

The blooms must all be fully developed, because the oil at this time contains the maximum amount of esters. Harvesting should be carried out rapidly – the cutting managed in a week if possible – so long as the weather is dry and there is no wind, the morning and evening of a fine day being particularly favourable to the flower gathering, on account of the fact that a certain amount of the ester portion of the oil is dissipated by a hot sun, as is easily seen by the fact that the Lavender plantations, and all fields of aromatic plants, are most highly perfumed about mid-day. Further, if there is any wind, the mid-day is the time when it will be hottest and most saturated with moisture, thus easily taking up the more volatile and more soluble particles of the essential oil. Very cold weather prevents the development of esters and rain is fatal for harvesting. If rain or fog appears, cutting should cease and not be resumed till the sun shines again.

Drying your lavender

Following the advice of the most seasoned professionals, remember always to pick your lavender as soon as the flowers appear, making sure that you choose the morning or evening of a dry, sunny day. If you want to make a tisane, infusion or tincture (see pages 37 and 41) from the fresh flowers, this is the best time to do it; otherwise, you can simply dry the flowers.

For dried arrangements: tie the stems into small bunches with garden string or raffia, and hang them in a dry, airy place.

For loose lavender: lay the stems in trays in a well-aired room. Once dry, the flowers can be stripped from the stalks with your fingers, and piled into your favourite pot-pourri bowls.

Home
Sweet Home

There is nothing cloying about the fragrance of lavender. Its special virtues are those of purity and a piercing cleanliness, rather than of sweetness. It was Izaak Walton, author of the English classic *The Compleat Angler*, who

avowed, 'I long to be in a house where the sheets smell of lavender.'
He was, of course, dreaming of a home that was not only impeccably clean, but looked after with loving care and attention to detail. It's not so difficult to envisage such a place: the floors and furniture gleam from regular polishing with lavender-scented waxes; the air is scented with the aroma of lavender wafting from heaped bowls and hanging bunches of the dried flowers; and the household linen is tucked away in drawers and linen cupboards with little sachets of dried lavender flowers to deter moths and other household pests.

Lavender has been used to keep homes clean and fresh-smelling for centuries. We know that its name derives from the Roman *lavare* 'to wash', but it is just as interesting to note that the word 'lavendress' used to be the old name for a washerwoman. This eventually became the modern word 'laundress', In the Middle Ages, freshly washed laundry was spread over blossoming lavender bushes in the sun, to absorb the delicate perfume while it was drying.

Using lavender at home

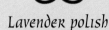

Lavender polish

Remove the lid from a tin of beeswax polish and let the wax soften for a while in a warm place. Then, using a toothpick, make several holes at regular intervals in the surface of the wax. Put one drop of essential oil of lavender into each of the holes, smooth the surface over with a cloth and replace the lid. The essential oil will permeate the wax, giving it a gorgeous fragrance.

To make home-made lavender polish you need:

- *570 ml white spirit*
- *110 g grated beeswax*
- *15 g grated olive oil-based soap*
- *350 ml of infused lavender flowers (page 37)*
- *essential oil of lavender*

Pour the white spirit into a bowl and add the beeswax and soap. Put the bowl in a warm spot (keep it away from naked flames). Leave for a couple of days or more, until the wax and soap are dissolved. Stir the mixture thoroughly. Bring the infusion to the boil, and pour it over the mixture. leave to cool, then stir well, blending the mixture into a creamy consistency. Finally, stir in several drops of essential oil of lavender, pour into a wide-necked container with a secure lid, and label.

Scented storage

Scenting your clothes and linen with lavender adds a touch of luxury to your life, but it also has a practical aspect. Lavender is very effective at deterring moths and other insect pests, so its use is invaluable anywhere where clothes are stored. There are various ways to do this; the most common is to make little sachets or bags filled with dried lavender flowers.

Flat sachets

You will need:

- *2 x 12 cm square pieces of printed cotton lawn, or organza*
- *embroidery thread and needle*
- *sewing thread*
- *dried lavender flowers*
- *essential oil of lavender*

Place the wrong sides of the fabric together and machine-stitch a narrow seam around three sides. Turn the sachet to the right side, and put in some lavender flowers. Don't over-fill the sachet, as the flowers will need to move around. Add a drop of essential oil, then close the open side with tiny slip-stitches. Decorate the edges of the sachet with a border of your favourite stitches.

'No sew' lavender bag

You will need:

- *scissors*
- *10 cm square piece of pretty fabric or plain muslin or organza*
- *dried lavender flowers*
- *essential oil of lavender*
- *matching sewing thread*
- *20 cm piece of ribbon*

Lay the fabric flat, and put a few dried lavender flowers in the centre. Add a drop of essential oil to the dried lavender. Gather up the sides of the fabric, wind several layers of cotton thread around it, then knot and snip the end. Conceal the thread by winding the ribbon around it, then finish with a decorative bow.

Scent your possessions

Once you've made your scented sachets, you can use them everywhere:

Keep them amongst the sheets, towels and other household linens in the airing cupboard to give them a wonderful, delicate scent.

Tuck them in your lingerie drawers to perfume your underwear.

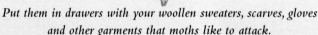

Put them in drawers with your woollen sweaters, scarves, gloves and other garments that moths like to attack.

Use the ribbon loops to hang lavender sachets and bags over the hooks of hangers to scent shirts and dresses.

Keep your shoes and boots fresh by tucking lavender bags, filled socks and sachets inside.

When you're storing items for winter, place sachets inside storage bags, and put them into the pockets of winter coats before zipping garment covers into place.

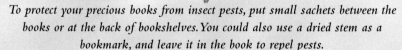

To protect your precious books from insect pests, put small sachets between the books or at the back of bookshelves. You could also use a dried stem as a bookmark, and leave it in the book to repel pests.

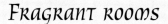

Fragrant rooms

A hint of lavender conjures up a soothing aura of peace and calm:

Use an aromatherapy burner to diffuse essential oil of lavender into the air.

Keep a shallow dish of lavender infusion (see page 37) on top of a radiator.

Keep the woody prunings near your hearth, and throw these on to the fire to scent the room.

Make stems into incense or 'smudge' sticks. Dissolve about 15 ml of saltpeter (available from chemists) in 225 ml of warm water for about 30 minutes. Soak the stems in this solution, then leave to dry out. Once lit, the sticks will smoulder slowly.

Scatter pretty, generously sized bowls around your home and fill them with dried lavender flowers. Refresh the flowers from time to time with a few drops of essential oil. Run your hands through your bowls occasionally to release the scent.

Hang a bunch of dried lavender stems from a hook in your kitchen to deter flies.

Tuck lavender-filled sachets inside cushion covers. If you have trouble getting to sleep, a sachet placed inside your pillow will help you to relax into a peaceful slumber.

Include spikes of lavender in vases, along with other cottage garden favourites, such as honeysuckle, roses, daisies, tansies, cornflowers and delphiniums. Or you might prefer using lavender on its own – with the dried stems heaped in a basket, for example, or arrayed in mathematical precision in a glass or galvanised metal container – simple, but chic.

Lavender bundles

You will need:

- *an odd number (11–13) of freshly picked lavender stems*
- *1 metre of lavender or blue satin ribbon*
- *scissors*
- *small safety pin*

Tie the stems into a neat bunch just below their heads with one end of the ribbon, knot the end securely, and trim the ribbon. Take the end of a stalk, then carefully bend it over the flower heads. Do this for each stem, to form a natural 'cage'. Bend the stems very gently to avoid snapping them. Once you have folded all the stalks over, attach the safety pin to the long end of the ribbon, then weave it in and out of the stalks to make a closely woven lattice pattern. Do this until you reach the base of the flower heads, then wind the ribbon around tightly. Fold in the short end of the ribbon if necessary, and tie the long end into a decorative bow. Finally, trim the ends of the stems to make an even edge, remove the safety pin from the ribbon, and trim.

Lavender's
Medicine Chest

Written records of the use of lavender for medicinal purposes can be traced back over two thousand years. It is this heritage of knowledgeable observation, based on practical trial and error, that has contributed the most useful health benefits to subsequent generations. Although much traditional botanical medical information has been threaded through with skeins of superstition and magical thinking, in many cases, the medicinal claims have, upon modern scientific testing, proved to be legitimate. This is certainly the case with lavender. The volatile oil in the plant does have antibiotic properties, and is highly effective in killing off many common bacteria. The oil contains over 200 compounds that have active antiseptic and anti-fungal properties.

How can lavender help you?

Lavender has been used to treat acne, anxiety, asthma, athlete's foot, boils, bronchitis, burns, chest infections, colds, colic, cystitis, depression, diarrhoea, ear infections, fainting, halitosis, headaches, hyperactivity, hysteria, indigestion, insomnia, hypertension (high blood pressure), insect bites and stings, mouth ulcers, nausea, nervous tension, migraine, muscle aches, rashes, rheumatism, scalds, sore gums, sunstroke, stress, throat infections and wind.

Because lavender is so powerful and versatile, it makes good sense to include it in your home medicine chest. It is also important to know how to use it safely and effectively. Your first task will be to obtain reliable, pesticide-free supplies. You can use lavender medicinally in two ways:

By making simple preparations from the fresh or dried whole flowers. These are recommended as being safe to take internally.

By using lavender's essential oil. This is a wonderfully convenient preparation, but it is important to note that, as with all essential oils, lavender oil should not be taken internally unless prescribed and supervised by a qualified herbal practitioner.

Please note that, although lavender is one of the safest natural remedies available, it should not be used in the very early stages of pregnancy.

Lavender Flowers

Preparations made from flowers of lavender are very safe for internal use – the species most popularly chosen for therapeutic purposes is *Lavandula officinalis*, also known as *Lavandula angustifolia*. If you enjoy growing plants, you can cultivate your own lavender, even if you don't have a garden – it will happily thrive in pots or window boxes. Otherwise, buy the dried flowers at your local health store, or herb supplier. Alternatively, you can log on to the websites of national lavender growing companies, and ask for details of their mail order facilities.

Making a simple infusion

If you've never made a herbal remedy at home before, you may have images of complicated procedures that involve turning your kitchen into an ancient apothecary's workshop. Making a herbal remedy is as easy as making a cup of tea. A simple cup of lavender tea (or tisane) can alleviate many of the ailments mentioned.

To make lavender tea, you'll need:

- *fresh or dried lavender flowers*
- *hot water (some people prefer to use mineral or filtered water)*
- *a tea ball (a small metal or ceramic infuser used for loose tea)*
- *1 teaspoon honey (optional)*

Put the water on to boil, and fill the tea ball with lavender flowers. Fasten the top of the ball, and put it in a cup. Pour the boiling water over the tea ball and fill the cup. Allow the mixture to infuse for 4–5 minutes, or even longer if you want a stronger brew. Remove the tea ball, and, if you like your tea to taste a little sweet, add a teaspoon of honey.

How to use lavender's healing powers

The healing properties of lavender tea can be employed in various ways.

An anti-bacterial agent

The tea can help if you are suffering from a bronchial chest infection caused by bacteria. It is also effective in combating throat infections, cystitis and diarrhoea caused by bacteria in food. It can also help with gum infections and mouth ulcers. If you have a sore throat, try gargling with the cooled tea to fight the infection.

A nerve-calming and anti-spasmodic agent

Lavender tea is good for colic (dilute the tea to 25 per cent normal strength for babies), indigestion, nausea, hypertension, migraine (take it at the first sign of an attack), nervous tension, stress and wind.

An analgesic and anti-inflammatory agent

Lavender tea can help to alleviate aches and pains, such as rheumatism, arthritis, and inflamed joints and muscles. You can also complement this gentle internal therapy with external treatments and applications (see below).

A sedative agent

Drinking a cup of lavender tea before going to bed can help you to get a good night's sleep if you suffer from insomnia. It is also very useful in combating hyperactivity and hysteria.

A tonic agent

Used in stronger-strength brews, lavender tea can also act as a reviving tonic. For instance, if you are going through a temporary patch of depression, it can help to lift your spirits.

Using infusions externally

As lavender is readily absorbed through the skin, there are other ways to use infusions. For example, you can make hot and cold compresses to apply direct to the body. Cold compresses are excellent for soothing headaches, bringing down fevers and calming irritated skin. Hot compresses are mostly helpful in treating aching joints and muscles, sprained limbs, neuralgia, cystitis and painful periods.

To make enough infusion for a compress:

- *40 g fresh or 20 g dried lavender flowers*
- *500 ml water*

Put the flowers into a basin. Boil the water and pour it over the flowers. Stir well, let the mixture stand for about 15 minutes, then strain the infusion into a separate container. Use the infusion hot or cold as necessary.

Applying a compress

Soak a clean flannel in the infusion, then wring it out thoroughly. Fold the flannel into a neat, flat shape, then apply it to the affected part. If you're using a hot compress, cover it with a piece of plastic film (clingfilm is fine), then place a pre-warmed towel on top to keep the heat in. Ideally, you should lie down under a blanket for about two hours to get the maximum benefit. Both hot and cold compresses should be re-soaked and re-applied at frequent intervals.

Steam inhalations

Inhaling the steam of a hot lavender infusion can bring wonderful relief when you have a feverish cold, a respiratory infection, a badly aching head, an infected throat, or inflamed sinuses. It is also a great way to release accumulated tension.

The method is simple: just pour the hot infusion into a bowl, drape a towel over your head, and quietly inhale the steam, letting it circulate gently throughout your body. After 10 to 15 minutes, rinse your face with tepid water, then, finally, splash with cold water. (Please note: people with asthma and heart conditions are advised not to use steam inhalations.)

A simple tincture

Another lavender medicine that will keep for a long time in your refrigerator is called a tincture, and, as it is quite strong compared to an infusion, you should follow the recommended dosage.

To make lavender tincture you'll need:

- *200 g dried flowers or 400 g fresh stems and flowers (chopped small)*
- *1 litre alcohol*
  *(60 per cent proof vodka or brandy is ideal) Other forms of alcohol, such as methylated spirit or ethyl alcohol, are not suitable and **must not** be used.*

Put the lavender in a clean glass jar with a tightly fitting lid, and pour in the alcohol. Keep the jar in a warm place in your kitchen, and shake it twice a day for two weeks. Then strain the mixture into a jug (it's a good idea to use a coffee filter to do this). Finally, using a funnel, decant this tincture into dark-coloured, airtight, clean glass bottles. Label them clearly, and store them in the refrigerator.

To use the tincture, simply dilute one teaspoonful in a little water. The recommended maximum is three doses a day. Use the tincture for the same problems that are alleviated by lavender tea (see page 37) – but don't give it to babies, as it is too strong.

Essential oil of lavender

The wonderful healing properties of lavender derive entirely from the action of the plant's essential oil.

This is usually extracted from the plant by passing steam through it while it is laid on grids. The process releases the oil's vapours from the glands, and these are collected into tanks as the steam cools.

You would need an enormous amount of lavender to make just a tiny amount of essential oil, so this is not practical to try at home. Fortunately, however, lavender oil is both affordable and accessible. Good quality products are available from a wide range of sources, including large pharmacies, local chemists, supermarkets and health stores.

Nowadays, essential oil of lavender is a 'must-have' home medication for thousands of people. It is highly convenient, of course, but just as important, it is also one of the safest of all oils to use – so safe, it can be used undiluted.

The best known modern legend about lavender's healing properties is the experience of the French chemist René Maurice Gattefosse. He burned his hand while working in the laboratory at his father's perfume factory, and impulsively plunged it into the nearest container of neat lavender oil to cool it. This immediately eased the pain, and he was not only amazed at the speed with which his hand healed, but also at the lack of infection or scarring. Anyone who has burned themselves on a hot iron or oven knows how long it usually takes for the scar to fade.

This experience triggered the chemist's subsequent investigations into the medicinal qualities of essential oils, which became the foundation of his revolutionary work on aromatherapy. He discovered that, because the molecules in essential oils are so small, they are rapidly absorbed into the body through the skin and nostrils, and this unlocks the plant's unique therapeutic effects.

Choosing your oil

You should always look for 100 per cent essential oil (some are sold in diluted form as aromatherapy oils), and check that the oil is a good quality, reputable brand. If it seems unusually inexpensive, the low price may simply be reflecting its inferior quality.

The oil is sold in a small, dark glass bottle, with a dispenser fixed at the mouth to control the flow of the oil, one drop at a time. The bottle should be stored in a cool, dark place – but not in a refrigerator. Properly stored, an essential oil can be effective for years. However, once it is diluted in a 'carrier' such as almond oil, its 'life span' is reduced to a couple of months!

Using essential oil of lavender

There are two ways to use essential oil of lavender. You can apply it directly on to your skin in undiluted form, or you can use it diluted in a carrier oil. Almond oil is popular as a carrier, but you can also use grapeseed, olive, carrot, evening primrose, peach or apricot kernel oil – whichever is your favourite. The usual dilution formula is to add 25 drops of pure essential oil to 50 ml of carrier oil.

First-aid: For immediate relief, apply neat lavender essential oil on insect bites, stings, minor cuts, grazes and bruises, small burns and scalds. To protect a cut, put 2 drops of essential oil on to the pad of a plaster before applying. This will prevent infection and speed healing.

Neuralgia and toothache: To calm the pain and inflammation, put 1–2 drops of neat lavender oil on to your fingertip, and gently rub it into the affected area.

Athlete's foot: Soak your feet in a tepid foot bath to which you've added 6 drops of essential oil of lavender. You can also apply neat oil between the infected toes, using a cotton bud.

Coughs, colds and catarrh: Rub diluted oil of lavender on to your chest. Alternatively, add 5 drops of essential oil to 500 ml of hot water and use as a steam inhalation, as described above.

Headache: Rub diluted oil on to your temples to ease the pain and tension of a headache.

Period pains: Gently massage your abdomen with diluted lavender oil, using circular movements, for about 10 minutes. Then apply a water bottle to the affected area for 30 minutes.

Muscle and joint pain: Massage aching joints and muscles with diluted lavender oil. Or use it to make a compress (see the instructions above) by adding 5 drops to 500 ml of hot water.

Stress buster: Add up to 6 drops of pure essential lavender oil to your warm bath water and swirl it around. Then get in the bath, lie back and relax. Use the same mix in children's baths; this will calm them when they're over-excited or irritable.

A calm environment: Use a few drops of lavender essential oil in an aromatherapy oil burner to fill the air around you with lavender's calming molecules, helping you to relax and to restore your emotional balance.

Follow the safety instructions on using your burner, and top up the water regularly so that the bowl never dries out. Always remember to extinguish the burner before going to sleep.

Sleep enhancer: Sprinkle up to 4 drops of pure essential lavender oil on to the corner of your pillow and inhale the aroma. Or dab a few drops on a tissue or a cotton wool ball to hold in your hand.

Spot attack: Use the tip of a cotton bud to apply neat lavender oil to spots; do this every morning and evening. You can also make a lavender face wash from 1 litre distilled water mixed with 5 drops of pure lavender essential oil. Soak a cotton wool ball in this lotion, and dab it over your face – it's both antiseptic and soothing.

Sunburn rescue: Dab your skin with the lavender wash described above, or make a soothing gel to cool you down.

Mix 5 drops of pure lavender essential oil with 5 ml aloe vera gel in the palms of your hands. Smooth this over the affected area.

Tired feet: A few drops of the essential oil in a comfortably hot foot bath will relax your feet and ease the fatigue from the rest of your body.

Lavender
For Beauty

In recent years, lavender has acquired a completely new image in the world of cosmetics, beauty products and perfumes. It may have been associated with demure maiden aunts in the past, but that certainly isn't the case nowadays. Lavender's clean, fresh scent has just the right appeal for 'no fuss'

modern tastes. Its essential oil has always been a precious ingredient in professional perfume-, soap- and cologne-making – it is grown in such profusion in Provence to supply the demands of the world-famous perfume-makers of Grasse.

Pure essential oil of lavender has its own kind of perfection, however; and, in using it for your personal beauty care, you are unlocking its unique alchemy. Lavender acts in two ways: on the deepest levels, it helps to keep every part of your body healthy and relaxed; and as a beauty product, it cleanses, scents and stimulates your skin. The delicious fragrance of lavender has astonishing properties in itself: it triggers your nervous system to produce an endorphin – a natural relaxant and mood-enhancing chemical that makes you feel (and therefore look) your very best. The effect of the essential oil upon your system is fast and direct, because it is rapidly absorbed into the skin and into your bloodstream. It contains components that improve your immune system, destroy bacteria and act as powerful antioxidants – the latter play an important part in helping to delay the effects of ageing. Moreover, these properties are long-lasting: molecules of lavender essential oil can be detected in the body up to seven hours after they have been absorbed.

Lavender in your beauty routine

Lavender not only keeps you looking radiant and healthy, it's also very easy and pleasant to use. Incorporate the following ideas into your beauty care routine, and you'll soon appreciate the benefits that this tiny flower can bring you.

Bath time

A daily bath in water that is scented with lavender will do wonders, both for your skin and sense of well-being. If you have plentiful supplies of the dried flowers, you can make a simple bath bag to hang under the hot water tap.

Simply cut out a 16 cm square of muslin and fill the centre with dried lavender buds. Another option is to mix equal quantities of lavender flowers and fine oatmeal (the latter is a highly effective skin softener). Gather the edges together, and secure the bag with a piece of ribbon. Leave enough ribbon to make a loop to hang over the tap. Then, as the hot water runs over the bag, it will fill your bath with lavender's beautiful perfume.

You may find it more convenient to keep a bottle of lavender essential oil by the bath and simply add a few drops to the bath water. You can also experiment with complementary scents, and make simple blends using other essential oils.

One easy method is to pour a little runny honey into the palm of your hand, then add 2 drops of lavender essential oil and 2 drops of mandarin essential oil. Swirl this around in the bath water – the honey emulsifies the oils and disperses them throughout the water. Another combination is 2 drops of lavender essential oil with 2 drops of geranium essential oil. These combinations make heavenly bath oils.

Face and body cleansing

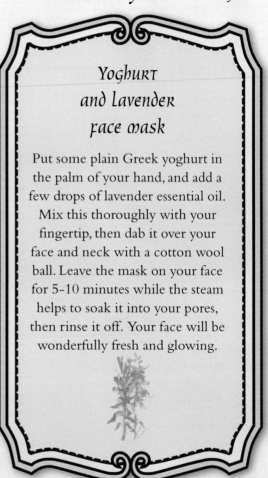

Yoghurt and lavender face mask

Put some plain Greek yoghurt in the palm of your hand, and add a few drops of lavender essential oil. Mix this thoroughly with your fingertip, then dab it over your face and neck with a cotton wool ball. Leave the mask on your face for 5-10 minutes while the steam helps to soak it into your pores, then rinse it off. Your face will be wonderfully fresh and glowing.

Oatmeal and lavender facial scrub

To make a gentle, scented and deep cleansing facial scrub, pour some fine oatmeal into the palm of your hand. Mix it to a runny paste with some water, and add a few drops of lavender essential oil. Now dab the oatmeal and lavender mixture all over your face and neck with a cotton wool ball, rub it lightly into your skin with your fingertips, then rinse off with clean water.

Lavender and witch hazel skin cleanser

This will keep your skin scrupulously clean and helps to prevent spots. Mix 12 drops of lavender and 12 drops of rose essential oil with 25 ml witch hazel and 75 ml distilled water. Shake well and store in a screw-top bottle. Apply every night with a cotton wool ball to remove all traces of makeup.

Lavender Beauty Soap

Here's an easy way to make some prettily scented little soaps.

- *25 g dried lavender flowers*
- *150 g bar Castile soap, finely grated*
- *350 ml lavender infusion (page 37)*
- *4 drops lavender essential oil*

Crush the flowers to a powder in a pestle and mortar. Melt the soap and infusion in a bowl placed over a saucepan of hot water, stirring occasionally until smooth. Remove the bowl from the pan, allow the mixture to cool a little, then stir in the crushed flowers and essential oil. Pour the soap mixture into small oiled food moulds (heart shapes are pretty) and leave these in a cool place to set. After a few days, remove the soap from the moulds, wrap each one in tissue paper, and store in a dry cupboard for 30 days before using.

Baking soda and lavender blackhead remover

These annoying 'plugs' of hardened sebaceous oils are often hard to loosen; but there is an easy and effective method. Combine 1 teaspoonful of baking soda and 1 teaspoonful of water on a saucer, add 3 drops of lavender oil, and mix well. Then rub the mixture gently on to the affected area of your face for 2–3 minutes. Rinse with warm water, then gently remove the blackhead. When you have done this, apply a drop of lavender oil on to the skin, to protect it from infection.

Healthy hair

Use lavender to keep your hair beautifully healthy and shining. It helps to regulate the activity of sebaceous glands, cleanses the scalp of any bacterial infection and dandruff, and is also reputed to stimulate hair growth.

To make a simple lavender hair cleanser, mix together 2–3 drops of lavender pure essential oil with a teaspoonful of very mild pH neutral shampoo. This mixture is so gentle that you can use it every day.

To condition your hair afterwards, either mix 2–3 drops of essential oil into a palmful of your usual conditioner, or add them to the water of your final rinse.

Sea salt and lavender body scrub:

An all-over body scrub makes you tingle with freshness from top to toe. Stand in the bath or shower and cover a sisal mitt or rough flannel with a generous layer of sea salt. Add several drops of lavender essential oil, then rub yourself all over. Use brisk, vigorous strokes to get your circulation going. Finally, have a lukewarm (not hot) shower, or rinse yourself thoroughly in the bath.

Skin moisturising

Most chemists or supermarkets sell inexpensive, 'own-brand', unperfumed moisturisers and lotions. These are often good quality products that are ideal for 'customizing' with pure lavender essential oil.

Just add 15 drops of pure lavender essential oil to every 50 ml of the cream. If you want to make the moisturiser look really pretty, add a drop of lavender or pink food colouring. Stir the cream thoroughly to blend in the oil, and store it in a glamorous cosmetic jar. This 'boosted' formula not only moisturises your skin, it also protects it from infection and combats the effects of ageing with antioxidants.

Hands and feet moisturiser

Your hands and feet can get a lot of wear and tear during the day – simple activities like washing up, housework and gardening all take their toll. And if you've been on your feet all day, the discomfort can be highly stressful.

To keep your hands and feet in peak condition, buy an inexpensive, unperfumed hand or body lotion from a chemist or supermarket. Add 10 drops of pure lavender essential oil for every 50 ml of the lotion and shake well. Smooth a little of this lotion on your hands and feet every night.

Firming and Toning

After a relaxing lavender bath, regular massage of your body with lavender essential oil diluted in your favourite carrier oil is a great way to help keep yourself toned. It is also believed to improve new cell growth, and gives your skin a smoother surface by speeding up the elimination of old skin cells. To make the oil, add 25 drops of pure lavender essential oil to 50 ml of a carrier oil (see page 43).

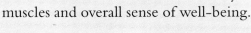

Using firm, sweeping movements, rub the oil all over your body.
Lie on a fluffy towel and cover yourself with another, then relax
and breathe quietly and deeply for a couple of minutes.
Do this once a week – it does wonders for your skin,
muscles and overall sense of well-being.

Scents, spritzes and toilet waters

Traditional lavender water

You will need:

- *600 g fresh lavender flowers*
- *1 litre mineral water*

Put the flowers into a large, clean, glass screw-top jar and stand a metal serving spoon in the jar to prevent the glass from cracking. Heat the water (but don't boil it) and pour it over the flowers. Stir thoroughly, remove the spoon, screw the cap on tightly, and leave the jar in direct sunlight for 24 hours. Filter the lavender flowers out by pouring the mixture through a coffee filter paper, then transfer the flower water into an atomizer or clean glass bottle.

Keep the mixture in the refrigerator and use it generously – it has no preservative, and won't keep for more than 7–10 days.

Lavender toilet vinegar

This is a classic freshener, ideal to dab on to your forehead and wrists on a sweltering summer's day. You will need:

- *475 ml white wine vinegar*
- *150 g fresh lavender flowers*

Put the vinegar and flowers into a clear glass screw-top jar. Close the cap tightly, and place the jar in direct sunlight for two weeks. Shake the mixture every 3–4 days. After a fortnight, strain the toilet vinegar through a coffee filter paper into a pretty glass bottle with a glass or cork stopper. You can tint the liquid with a few drops of lavender or pink food colouring if you like.

Citrus skin spritz

You will need:

- 10 ml inexpensive vodka
- 3 drops pure lavender essential oil
- 3 drops pure mandarin essential oil
- 1 drop pure rose essential oil
- 200 ml mineral water

Mix the ingredients together. Shake well, and transfer the mixture to an atomizer. Keep it in the refrigerator. This makes a great freshener when you're tired in hot weather and need a fast boost.

Eau de toilette

You will need:

- 25 drops essential oil
- 50 ml vodka

Shake the vodka and essential oil together in a screw-top bottle, and leave to infuse for a couple of days. Then decant the eau de toilette into a dark glass bottle with an airtight lid or stopper. (A small funnel is useful when doing this.) Treasure every one of your marvellous creations, and enjoy wearing them.

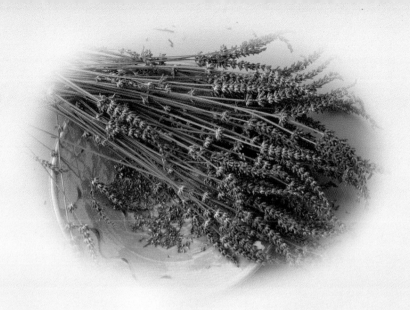

A Taste of Lavender

Lavender has played an important part in culinary history for centuries. For instance, it was widely used during Tudor and Elizabethan times as an ingredient in a variety of dishes, and, as has been mentioned, was a particular favourite of Queen Elizabeth I. She let it be known that she could not eat her roast lamb without an accompaniment of her favourite lavender jelly. The owners of great country houses throughout the land were advised to have plenty of lavender growing in their gardens.

Lavender has a wonderful affinity with various meats: if you normally use thyme or rosemary when you're roasting or grilling lamb, pork or chicken, simply halve the usual quantity and make up the difference with lavender.

Never be timid about using lavender in your cooking – it is a delightfully versatile ingredient that combines beautifully with herbs such as rosemary and thyme. And if you can obtain fresh flowers and herbs, so much the better. As a rough guide, 1 teaspoon of dried herb is equivalent to 1 tablespoon of fresh.

Please note that the species of lavender recommended for culinary use is *Lavandula angustifolia* (also known as *Lavandula officinalis*), and that you must always use lavender that is **entirely free of pesticides**.

You may have eaten lavender already, without being aware of it. The flower is a key ingredient in the aromatic mixture *Herbes de Provence*; this is widely available from supermarkets, and is added to wine-based casseroles, daubes and braises that require slow, gentle simmering.

Traditional lavender jelly

- *1 kg chopped cooking or crab apples*
- *400 ml water*
- *150 ml white wine vinegar*
- *a handful of fresh (or half a handful of dried) lavender flowers*
- *sugar, as below*

Put the apples, water and white wine vinegar in a large pan, and bring to the boil. Add the lavender flowers, and simmer gently until the apples are soft. Strain the mixture through a jelly bag overnight. The following day, measure the juice, pour it into a saucepan, and add 350 g of sugar for each 575 ml of juice. Stir well, then let the mixture boil until it thickens (but don't let it boil over). Cool the jelly for 10 minutes, strain through a fine sieve, then pour into clean jars. Label clearly, and keep the lavender jelly in a cool, dark place.

Salads and dressings

Scatter a handful of fresh flower buds over summer salads of mixed leaves and other edible flowers. Make a simple lavender-flavoured oil to use in your salad dressings. Pour about 300 ml of sunflower or safflower oil into a clear glass jar, and fill it with fresh lavender flowers. Cover the top with muslin and place it in a sunny spot. Leave the oil to infuse for about 2 weeks, stirring it daily. Finally, strain the oil through the muslin and decant into a clean, airtight bottle and store in a cool, dark place.

Sweet lavender delights

Lemon and lavender dessert jelly

You will need:

- *Packet of lemon flavoured jelly cubes (choose a good brand made with real lemon juice)*
- *lavender infusion (see page 37)*

Read the instructions to check how much liquid is needed to dissolve the jelly. Use half the quantity of water, and make up the remaining half with a lavender infusion. Heat the water and infusion in a pan, pour it over the jelly, stir, and leave to cool. Serve the jelly with fresh cream and lemon slices.

Lavender honey

If you enjoy honey on toast, crumpets or with your breakfast yoghurt, try this for a special treat. Put 250 g runny honey into a double boiler and heat it very gently. Stir a handful of fresh lavender buds into the warmed honey, and keep it over a very low heat for 15–20 minutes. Remove from the heat and let the honey cool before straining into a clean, screw-top glass jar.

Lavender Lemonade

This is wonderfully cooling and calming on hot summer days.

- *600 ml water*
- *25 g white sugar*
- *juice of 1 lemon*
- *handful of fresh lavender flowers*

Put all the ingredients in a saucepan, and heat gently until all the sugar is dissolved. Leave the mixture to cool in the refrigerator for at least 2–3 hours, or overnight. To serve, strain the lemonade, then pour into tall glasses over lots of ice cubes. Decorate with lemon slices and sprigs of lavender.